The Magic Stairs

A Personal Journal to Reveal the Wisdom of your Heart

Laura Dunn

THE MAGIC STAIRS

A Personal Journal to Reveal the Wisdom of Your Heart

By Laura Dunn

Address:
Transcendent Publishing
PO Box 66202
St. Pete Beach, FL 33736
www.TranscendentPublishing.com

Transcendent
——Publishing——

ISBN-10: 0-9993125-2-9
ISBN-13: 978-0-9993125-2-0

Printed in the United States of America.

Dedication

This journal and my new creative experiences are dedicated to a charming, beautiful and loving soul. From the moment he was born, his dark brown eyes captivated me and opened my heart, allowing myself to see the world in a whole new perspective. Twenty-one years later, I am still captivated. He has the capacity to look at others and see the light that shines within them, no matter the outward circumstances. He stands strong in his truth with grace. This is my son, Taylor.

Our relationship is such a joy; he has been a great teacher and will continue to be as each of our lives unfold. His sense of humor and entertaining impressions never fails to make me laugh. He created one of the messages in *The Magic Stairs* personal guidance card deck and is quick to remind me of this when need be!

He inspires me to ignite a passion in others. A passion they have yet to know. I eagerly await to see his spark coming to light.

So with that being said, my heart will continue to smile every time his deep brown eyes look back at mine. Thank you, Taylor.

Love Always

The beautiful writer
of this
Magic Stairs Journal is

_____

(Name)

Within the creation of this journal, I write from the heart. My voice speaks in handwritten words. Whether I know it or not I am ready to step into a new realm. I journey in, and I journey out. I will deepen what inspires me, become aware of my beliefs and have the courage to change. With the interconnectedness of writing and healing, I will gain clarity, identify patterns and solutions, and become that of higher consciousness. Within these pages are self-love and love for others. My expressions here are perfect. Heartache, loss, the unknown, vulnerability, doubt, anticipations, wonder and fun are all welcome here. It is safe to be all emotions written, for this is my story. I write from the heart, and I write with purpose. My wisdom emerges.

The Magic Stairs Journal

After writing in your journal, you may choose to silently do a personal meditation with the following passage or at any time listen to the guided meditation available on the website:

The Magic Stairs

www.soulfireenterprise.com

Close your eyes, walk up the Magic Stairs and step into the Light.

The Divine will assist you in revealing the wisdom of your own heart.

Feel tiny sparks of brilliant colors through your entire body.

Ask Spirit for further guidance on all you have just expressed in your personal journal.

Allow yourself to observe what naturally unfolds.

When you are ready, thank Spirit that this guidance will be revealed in the perfect Divine time,

And that you will integrate that energy into your being.

This Magic will burst light into the Universe.

Explore

Exploring your emotions can open the door to a positive, healthy process. Identify your feelings and receive the eye-opening indispensable messages.

_____

_____

_____

_____

_____

_____

_____

_____

_____

_____

_____

_____

_____

_____

_____

_____

_____

_____

_____

I express my never ending potential

_____

_____

_____

_____

_____

_____

_____

_____

_____

_____

_____

_____

_____

_____

_____

_____

_____

_____

_____

_____

Miracles are within me

_____
_____
_____
_____
_____
_____
_____
_____
_____
_____
_____
_____
_____
_____
_____
_____
_____
_____
_____
_____
_____

I am open to grow spiritually

_____

_____

_____

_____

_____

_____

_____

_____

_____

_____

_____

_____

_____

_____

_____

_____

_____

_____

Not knowing something gives me the opportunity to learn

_____

_____

_____

_____

_____

_____

_____

_____

_____

_____

_____

_____

_____

_____

_____

_____

_____

_____

_____

_____

_____

_____

_____
_____
_____
_____
_____
_____
_____
_____
_____
_____
_____
_____
_____
_____
_____
_____
_____
_____
_____
_____
_____
_____
_____
_____
_____
_____

I participate in enriching experiences

_____

_____

_____

_____

_____

_____

_____

_____

_____

_____

_____

_____

_____

_____

_____

_____

_____

_____

_____

_____

_____

My relationships are healthy and loving

_____

_____

_____

_____

_____

_____

_____

_____

_____

_____

_____

_____

_____

_____

_____

_____

_____

_____

_____

_____

_____

Sacred Space

Sacred space is anywhere you desire to design your own sanctuary.
Whether it be in your visualization or physical surroundings.
It is as unique as you. Spend intentional daily time there.

Sometimes the Divine has a different plan than my own

I am worth loving

_____

_____

_____

_____

_____

_____

_____

_____

_____

_____

_____

_____

_____

_____

_____

_____

_____

_____

_____

_____

_____

New and wonderful opportunities unfold

Creativity surges through me

_____

_____

_____

_____

_____

_____

_____

_____

_____

_____

_____

_____

_____

_____

_____

_____

_____

_____

_____

I am clear about what I desire

_____
_____
_____
_____
_____
_____
_____
_____
_____
_____
_____
_____
_____
_____
_____
_____
_____
_____
_____

I am completely supported by the Universe

_____

_____

_____

_____

_____

_____

_____

_____

_____

_____

_____

_____

_____

_____

_____

_____

_____

_____

_____

Believe in Others

Serve others by believing in them. This will create a supporting energy they can call upon to build their dreams. Beautiful energy will return to you.

_____

_____

_____

_____

_____

_____

_____

_____

_____

_____

_____

_____

_____

_____

_____

_____

_____

Be still. Silence hears gifts

_____
_____
_____
_____
_____
_____
_____
_____
_____
_____
_____
_____
_____
_____
_____
_____
_____
_____
_____
_____

I have supporting friends

_____

_____

_____

_____

_____

_____

_____

_____

_____

_____

_____

_____

_____

_____

_____

_____

_____

_____

_____

_____

I choose wisely

_____

_____

_____

_____

_____

_____

_____

_____

_____

_____

_____

_____

_____

_____

_____

_____

_____

_____

_____

_____

My heart always tells me

_____

_____

_____

_____

_____

_____

_____

_____

_____

_____

_____

_____

_____

_____

_____

_____

_____

_____

_____

_____

_____

_____

_____

_____

_____

_____

I dance with the Universe

_____
_____
_____
_____
_____
_____
_____
_____
_____
_____
_____
_____
_____
_____
_____
_____
_____
_____
_____
_____
_____
_____

See the magnificence in others

_____

_____

_____

_____

_____

_____

_____

_____

_____

_____

_____

_____

_____

_____

_____

_____

_____

_____

_____

_____

Keepers of the Soul

Never are we alone. Our Keepers of the soul walk beside us at all times. Thank them. Give gratitude. Invite them to assist you. These Guardians are fundamental to our existence.

Signs and symbols are placed on my path

_____
_____
_____
_____
_____
_____
_____
_____
_____
_____
_____
_____
_____
_____
_____
_____
_____
_____
_____
_____

I accept my lessons and expand

_____
_____
_____
_____
_____
_____
_____
_____
_____
_____
_____
_____
_____
_____
_____
_____
_____
_____
_____

I go beyond limited thinking

_____

_____

_____

_____

_____

_____

_____

_____

_____

_____

_____

_____

_____

_____

_____

_____

_____

_____

_____

_____

_____

_____

_____

_____

_____

_____

_____

_____

_____

_____

_____

_____

_____

_____

_____

_____

_____

_____

_____

_____

_____

_____

_____

_____

LAURA DUNN

I am a magnet for all good experiences

_____
_____
_____
_____
_____
_____
_____
_____
_____
_____
_____
_____
_____
_____
_____
_____
_____
_____
_____

I lovingly take care of my physical body

_____
_____
_____
_____
_____
_____
_____
_____
_____
_____
_____
_____
_____
_____
_____
_____
_____
_____
_____

_____

_____

_____

_____

_____

_____

_____

_____

_____

_____

_____

_____

_____

_____

_____

_____

_____

_____

_____

_____

_____

_____

_____

_____

_____

_____

_____

I follow my intuition and find the answers I need

_____

_____

_____

_____

_____

_____

_____

_____

_____

_____

_____

_____

_____

_____

_____

_____

_____

_____

I ask and let go

I am empowered and confident

_____

_____

_____

_____

_____

_____

_____

_____

_____

_____

_____

_____

_____

_____

_____

_____

_____

_____

_____

Commander of the Flame

Continue to keep the flame lit that burns strong and bright within you. Allow your pioneering spirit to light the way for others. Endless possibilities will unfold.

I recognize the beauty in others

May others be blessed

_____
_____
_____
_____
_____
_____
_____
_____
_____
_____
_____
_____
_____
_____
_____
_____
_____
_____
_____
_____
_____
_____
_____
_____
_____
_____
_____
_____
_____

My voice sends waves to the Universe

Everything happens for my ultimate good

_____

_____

_____

_____

_____

_____

_____

_____

_____

_____

_____

_____

_____

_____

_____

_____

_____

_____

I radiate beauty and grace

_____
_____
_____
_____
_____
_____
_____
_____
_____
_____
_____
_____
_____
_____
_____
_____
_____
_____

I am at peace with all that has happened

_____

_____

_____

_____

_____

_____

_____

_____

_____

_____

_____

_____

_____

_____

_____

_____

_____

_____

It is easy for me to embrace change

_____

_____

_____

_____

_____

_____

_____

_____

_____

_____

_____

_____

_____

_____

_____

_____

_____

_____

_____

_____

_____

Communication with others flows effortlessly